FAST
DÉCOR

DÉC

ANNEMARIE MEINTJES
& KAREN ROOS

PHOTOGRAPHY BY

MASSIMO CECCONI

FAST
COR

CONTENTS

C O N T E N T S

This is a book of clever decorating tricks that will instantly brighten up your home. Some of these ideas are our own, while others we've picked up over the years photographing homes for magazines.

In the pages that follow, you'll find ideas on how to dress a naked light bulb while searching for the perfect chandelier, or how to display the family photo album without spending your inheritance on frames. You'll also discover the everyday magic of tea lights and the use of fairy lights beyond the Christmas tree. It's window-dressing rather than curtain making; creating

ABOUT THIS BOOK

accents with colour, using objects from nature and learning to rethink, recycle and revamp before you go out and spend money.

All in all it's about styling up your home for a party, a special guest's visit or for a photographic shoot. The best part is that it looks great and costs little enough to enable you to restyle it as often as you wish.

Annemarie Meintjes and Karen Roos

ONE
RETHINK

rethink *vb.* to think again about something (a plan, idea or system) in order to change or improve it

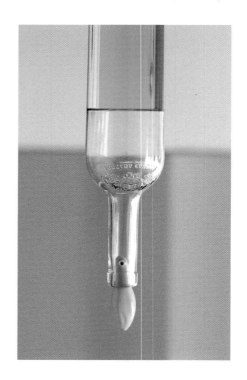

LOOK BEYOND THE ORIGINAL FUNCTION

IF THE SHAPE OF A CONTAINER PLEASES YOU, REMOVE THE BRANDING AND RECYCLE IT INTO

A CITRONELLA LANTERN, A VASE OR A DECANTER.

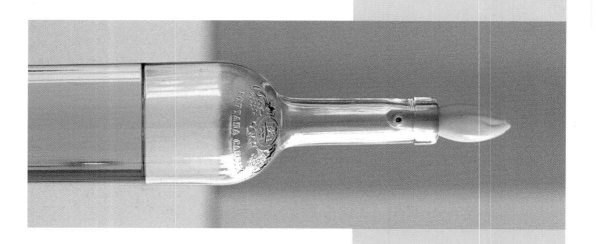

DE-BOXED

IF YOU THINK BOXED WINE IS NOT YOUR THING, THEN THINK AGAIN. ONCE EMPTY, THE BAG IN THE BOX TRANSFORMS INTO THE IDEAL SHAMPOO/BODY WASH DISPENSER FOR THE SHOWER. REMOVE THE BOX, RINSE AND IT'S READY TO GO. DE-BOXED, THE BAGS ALSO MAKE FUNKY SCATTER CUSHIONS WHEN INFLATED OR FILLED WITH POLYSTYRENE BALLS, SHREDDED PAPER OR PLASTIC.

WATCH THE
ORDINARY

BIN THE BOX,

BUT KEEP THE BAG

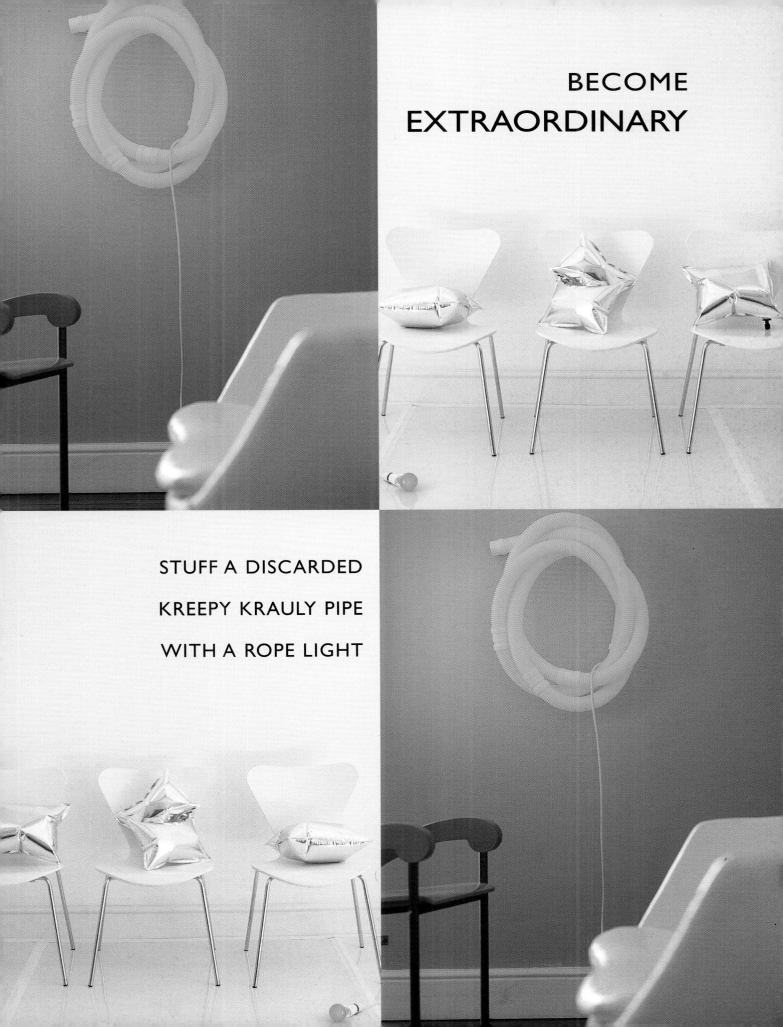

BECOME
EXTRAORDINARY

STUFF A DISCARDED
KREEPY KRAULY PIPE
WITH A ROPE LIGHT

RESCUE YOUR ROOM FROM A SHY AND RETIRING WALL FINISH

TO CREATE AN INSTANT AND SPECTACULAR WALL FINISH WITH A WONDERFUL IRIDESCENT GLOW, STICK POLYSTYRENE APPLE TRAYS AGAINST THE WALL, USING THE SILVER-GREEN FLIPSIDE ON THE OUTSIDE. LIGHT AS A FEATHER, THE TRAYS WILL STAY UP AGAINST THE WALL WITH TINY PIECES OF PRESTIK BUT, IF YOU PLAN TO KEEP THEM UP FOR A LONG PERIOD, THEN STICK THEM ON WITH DOUBLE-SIDED VELCRO SQUARES, WHICH WILL ALLOW YOU TO TAKE THEM DOWN FOR CLEANING.

APPLE TRAYS MEASURE 36 CM X 58 CM, SO YOU CAN WORK OUT HOW MANY YOU NEED AND RETRIEVE THEM FROM SUPERMARKET DEPOTS OR TEAM UP WITH FRIENDS TO ORDER A STASH DIRECTLY FROM THE SUPPLIER. THEY'RE GREAT FOR LOFTS, OFFICES AND EVEN KIDS' ROOMS AND STUDENTS' DIGS.

REINVENT EVERYDAY OBJECTS

AIRLINE-STYLE MEAL TRAYS HAVE BECOME THE ULTIMATE TABLEWARE FOR TREND-AWARE URBANITES. SHOP IN ARMY SURPLUS STORES FOR STAINLESS-STEEL VERSIONS.

ONE SHEET OF BUBBLE FOIL CEILING INSULATION PIERCED WITH THE GLOBES FROM A STRING OF FAIRY LIGHTS CREATES A TALKING POINT – ON A WALL OR AS A ROOM DIVIDER. FOR KIDS' ROOMS, BACK IT WITH ANOTHER SHEET AND SEAL THE SIDES TO CONTAIN THE FAIRY LIGHTS.

LATERAL THINKING = CREATIVE SPACES

LOVE AT FIRST LIGHT

TOO OFTEN THE MOST BEAUTIFUL ROOMS DECORATED WITH THE GREATEST OF CARE SHARE A COMMON TROUBLE SPOT – THE NAKED LIGHT BULB.

BUY THE BIGGEST LIGHT BULB YOU CAN FIND AND GO BARE, OR LOOK AROUND YOU FOR ORDINARY, UNEXPECTED ITEMS THAT CAN BE TURNED INTO LAMPSHADES. DRESS A BULB IN A HUMBLE FISHING BASKET AND CREATE A WORK OF ART.

FAST-TRACK
LIGHTING

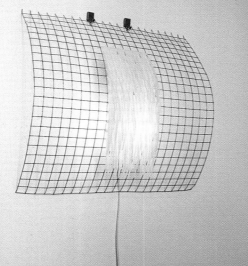

DRESS LIGHTS

CREATE A WALL LIGHT WITH METAL

MESH FENCING AND CABLE TIES

(DESIGNED TO TIE ELECTRICAL CABLES

TOGETHER AND ALSO USED BY

AIRPORT ATTENDANTS TO SEAL ZIPPER

BAGS). ALTERNATIVELY, YOU CAN STRIP

AN OLD LAMPSHADE AND TIE THE TAGS

TO THE FRAME.

MAKE LIGHT WORK OF IT

POLYPROPYLENE SHEETING IS SOLD BY THE METRE AND,

ONCE CUT, CURLS UP NATURALLY INTO A ROLL. SIMPLY

PLACE A LOW VOLTAGE LIGHT SOURCE IN THE CENTRE

OF THE ROLL TO MAKE A CYLINDRICAL LAMP.

ROLL PLAYING

DUMP THE
DOCUMENTS
AND STORE WINE
IN TUBES.

CUT TUBES MANUFACTURED FOR THE CARPET INDUSTRY TO SIZE AND TOP WITH A SHEET OF SANDBLASTED GLASS TO MAKE A GREAT TABLE.

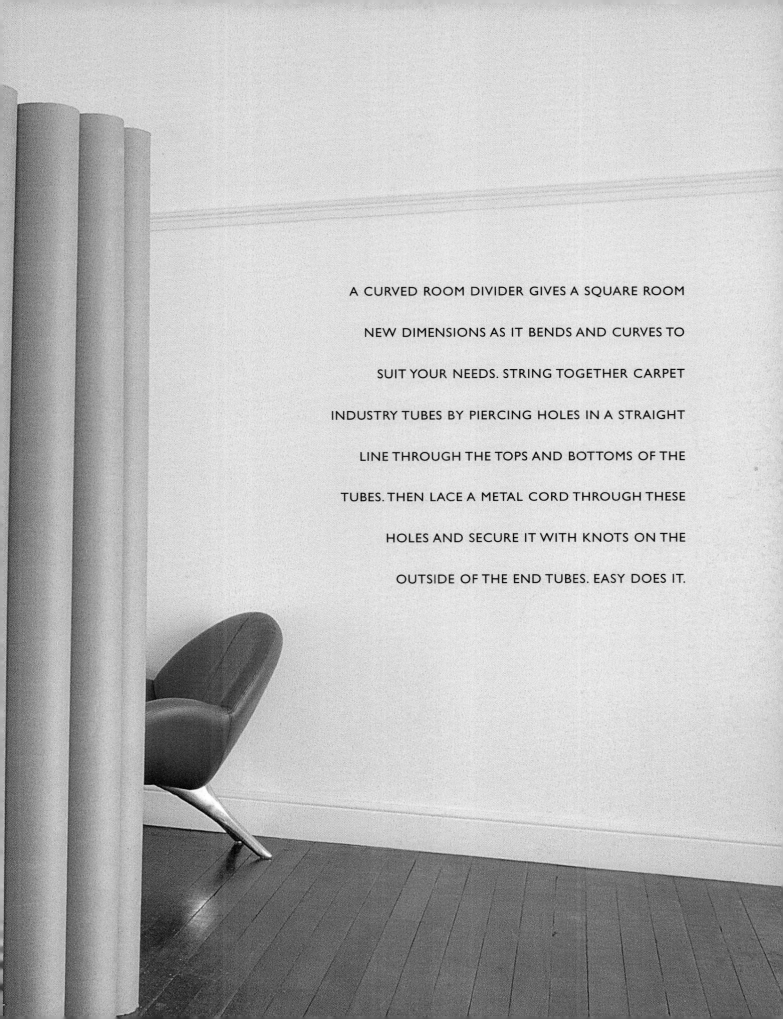

A CURVED ROOM DIVIDER GIVES A SQUARE ROOM

NEW DIMENSIONS AS IT BENDS AND CURVES TO

SUIT YOUR NEEDS. STRING TOGETHER CARPET

INDUSTRY TUBES BY PIERCING HOLES IN A STRAIGHT

LINE THROUGH THE TOPS AND BOTTOMS OF THE

TUBES. THEN LACE A METAL CORD THROUGH THESE

HOLES AND SECURE IT WITH KNOTS ON THE

OUTSIDE OF THE END TUBES. EASY DOES IT.

Ho il suono
dei tuoi
passi dau
il cuore

paper *n.* a substance made
from cellulose fibres derived
from rags, wood etc., and
formed into flat thin sheets
suitable for writing on,
decorating walls, wrapping, etc.

paper over *vb. (tr. adv.)*
to conceal (something
controversial or unpleasant)

WINDOW-DRESSING

SEE PAPER AS A

FIBRE. BUY IT BY THE

METRE AND FLAUNT IT.

IT'S THE INSTANT SOLUTION

FOR ROUND WINDOWS.

LIGHT IS LIFE

DRESS A WINDOW IN A

FLURRY OF POST-IT NOTES

SO YOU KEEP THE LIGHT

BUT BLOCK OUT

UNSAVOURY VIEWS.

PEG AND PAPER

ABOVE: SETTING A TABLE WITH

PAPER CAN BE GRAND.

LEFT: BUY A PRINTED GRAPHIC

IMAGE, THEN PEG IT, UNFRAMED,

ONTO A WALL WITH VELCRO

SQUARES FOR AN UNSTRUCTURED

LOOK THAT GIVES YOU THE

FREEDOM TO CHANGE THE IMAGE

TO SUIT YOUR MOOD.

PAPER CHANDELIER –
GIVE YOUR DOODLES WINGS

LUXURIATE IN A PAPER ROOM OF YOUR OWN

MAKING ... AS INSPIRED BY LIGHTING GURU INGO

MAURER'S 'ZETTEL'Z'.

FLIGHT
OF FANCY

CREATE A ROMANTIC MOOD WITH THE WELL-THUMBED

PAGES OF A LOVE STORY, INTERSPERSED WITH LOVE

NOTES AND POEMS.

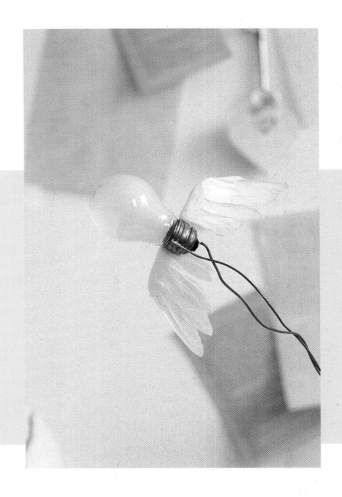

DUFAYLITE IS A LIGHTWEIGHT, FLEXIBLE HONEYCOMB CARDBOARD MATERIAL THAT IS USED COMMERCIALLY TO FILL DOORS. WHEN STRETCHED TO ITS LIMITS IT BECOMES A DESIGNER ROOM DIVIDER.

A LIGHT DRESSER

DUFAYLITE HAS THE RIGHT WEIGHT, THE RIGHT TEXTURE AND THE RIGHT

DELICATE, LACY LOOK. STRETCH IT OUT AND IT CONCERTINAS BACK.

IT CONCEALS AND ALSO REVEALS. IT CAN TRANFORM ITSELF INTO

ANYTHING, EVEN A DRESS! IT IS SOLD PER KILOGRAM, IN ROLLS

OR IN PIECES, AND CAN BE ORDERED TO SIZE.

THREE
COLOUR

colour *n.* a substance, such as
dye or paint, that imparts colour

colouring *n.* a false or
misleading appearance

CHARGE
YOUR HOUSE
WITH COLOUR

TWO-TONE TANGO

TAKE ONE COLOUR AND LAYER IT

TONE UPON TONE.

QUICK COLOUR FIX

USE COLOUR AS AN ACCENT TO BRIGHTEN UP YOUR SPACE. BUY A BOX OF THE SAME COLOUR FRUIT OR THE EVER-FRESH PAPER VERSION. TRAWL THE DEPTHS OF YOUR LOCAL FISHERMAN'S SUPPLY STORE FOR GREAT BOTTLE STOPPERS.

BUY COLOUR BY THE METRE OR DYE IT IN LOADS!

REINVENT OLD STALWARTS WITH DYE AND REVEL IN THE FACT THAT NO TWO ITEMS IN THE SAME LOAD WILL BE THE SAME SHADE BECAUSE OF THE ORIGINAL COLOUR AND FABRIC MIX. YOU CAN OPT FOR DIY IF IT'S A SMALL BUNDLE IN COTTON, LINEN OR SILK. IF IT'S A MIXED LOAD, LEAVE IT TO THE PROFESSIONALS.

LUCKY **DIP**

FAST
DÉCOR

CREATE YOUR OWN ROOM RECIPE

CHANGE THE COLOUR OF A ROOM BY PLAYING WITH COLOURED GLOBES, UPLIGHTERS,

DOWNLIGHTERS, SPOTS ... THE POSSIBILITIES ARE ENDLESS.

SUPER-FAST DÉCOR

DISPLAY EVERYTHING IN THE SAME COLOUR AND

STORE THE REST!

PLAY WITH STRIPES

INSTANT WALLPAPER: HANG STRIPS OF COLOURED

PLASTIC AT REGULAR INTERVALS ON THE WALLS. GLUE OR

STAPLE THE STRIPS TO THE PICTURE RAIL (OR CORNICE)

AND SKIRTING BOARDS.

PLAY WITH SPRAY PAINT

IGNORE MATT PAINTS, SHINE IS THE NEW THING. DON'T

WASTE TIME WITH REGULAR SPRAY PAINT, BUT GO FOR

METALLIC AUTO SPRAY PAINT WITH AN EXCITING RANGE

OF COLOURS THAT DRY HARD AND FAST.

COOL COLOURS – CLEVER WALLS

PAINT UPDATES, RENEWS AND EXCITES. TAKE IT BEYOND THE

WALLS TO WOOD STAINS AND METALLIC PAINTS.

THE FACT THAT YOU CAN TAKE A FASHION ITEM TO ALMOST

ANY HARDWARE STORE AND HAVE PAINT MIXED IN THE EXACT

SHADE IS WHY DECORATORS LOVE TO PAINT. THE FACT THAT

YOU CAN REPAINT IF YOU FIND YOU CAN'T LIVE WITH THE

COLOUR AFTER A WHILE IS WHY THEIR CLIENTS LOVE TO LIVE

OUT THEIR COLOUR FANTASIES.

DON'T BE SHOCKED – PERHAPS YOU SHOULD TRY A BLACK

ROOM NEXT.

nature *n.* (often cap.) the whole system of the existence, forces and events of all physical life that are not controlled by mankind

natural *adj.* of, existing in, or produced by nature

MAKE NATURE'S CALENDAR OUT OF A POCKET CURTAIN, THEN CHART THE SEASONS FROM FEATHERS TO LEAVES TO FLOWERS TO HOLLY.

STYLE ON A STRING

SEASONAL SOUVENIRS OR COUNTRY CUTTINGS

ADD AN AIR OF SPIRITUAL FREEDOM TO A SIMPLE

STRING CURTAIN. TIE STRINGS TO A FALLEN

BRANCH OR A PIECE OF DRIFTWOOD AND

REMEMBER TO TIE THE HEAVIER OBJECTS

TO THE LOWER ENDS OF EACH LENGTH TO

WEIGH THEM DOWN.

TACTILE TOUCHES TO MAKE YOU PURR

ADORN A ROUND SCATTER CUSHION OR BARSTOOL

WITH SUPER-SOFT WHITE OSTRICH FEATHERS.

DISPLAY YOUR STASH OF PORCUPINE QUILLS IN

AN ORIGINAL WAY.

DARE TO BE
DIFFERENT

THE SECRET HISTORY ...

... OF A WEATHERED SHELL GIVES AN OVAL MIRROR A ROMANTIC PAST.

BEAUTY BRANCHES OUT

DEAD BRANCHES HAVE BEAUTY – TAKE THEM INTO YOUR HOME AND

USE THEM AS CENTREPIECES ABOVE THE TABLE OR TURN THEM INTO

CHANDELIERS USING FAIRY LIGHTS OR HANGING TEA LIGHTS.

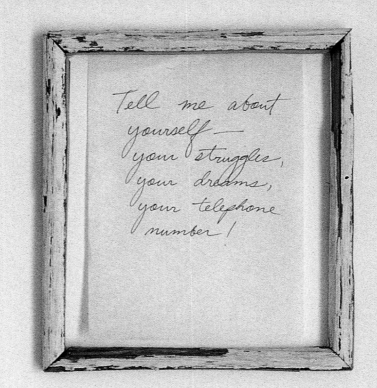

Tell me about
yourself—
your struggles,
your dreams,
your telephone
number!

BARK AS BIRD IN FLIGHT

ORGANICS ARE THE HEARTBEAT OF DESIGN. A PIECE

OF BARK GIVES MOVEMENT TO A STATIC WALL.

TREE TRUNKS AS TABLES

SAVE THE TREE TRUNKS! AND RECYCLE INTO

ROBUST SIDE TABLES.

COME BACK SLEEPERS

IN THE CURRENT MOOD OF ECO-AWARENESS, TEXTURES AND

SCULPTURAL FORMS LEAD THE WAY, MAKING THE RAILWAY SLEEPER THE

LOOK OF THE MOMENT. IT'S AN UNTREATED, WEATHERED, LAYERED AND

ORGANIC FEEL THAT IS ENHANCED BY THE SHAPES THAT SURROUND IT.

STRAW MATTRESSES OR CRISP LINEN COMPLIMENTS SLEEPERS AND

CREATES A FEELING OF SANCTUARY. KEEP THEM NATURAL AND TURN

THEM INTO A BED, A DAY BED OR EVEN A SUN BED ON THE DECK.

PURITY IS KEY.

FIVE
PHOTOGRAPHS

photographs *n.* images of
an object, person, scene, etc., in
the form of a print or slide
recorded by camera

photostat *n.* 1. *Trademark.* a
machine or process used to make
photographic copies of written,
printed or graphic matter
2. any copy made by
such a machine

YOU HAVE BEEN
FRAMED

FRAMING CAN BE PRICEY. CLEAR
CLIPBOARDS AND A4 SHEETS OF ACETATE
OFFER AN INEXPENSIVE SOLUTION.
ALTERNATIVELY, PHOTOSTAT THE IMAGES
ONTO ARCHITECT'S FILM OR A4 SHEETS OF
ACETATE. BOLD GRAPHIC IMAGES LOOK
GREAT AS ROOM DIVIDERS OR WINDOW
BLINDS WHERE YOU WANT TO RETAIN THE
LIGHT WITHOUT REVEALING THE VIEW.

LAID BACK LOUNGING WITH A FAMILY FOCUS

USING PHOTOGRAPHS OR PHOTOSTAT IMAGES TO DECORATE YOUR HOME IS A UNIQUE WAY OF PERSONALISING YOUR

SPACE. IT ALSO PROVIDES UNUSUAL SURFACES FOR DISPLAYING THE FAMILY ALBUM. PHOTOSTATS ARE INEXPENSIVE AND

VARY FROM A5 SIZE TO THE CLASSIC A0 POSTER SIZE. IT CAN BE DONE ON ANY COLOUR PAPER, ACETATE, ARCHITECT'S

FILM, FABRIC AND EVEN ON CROCKERY.

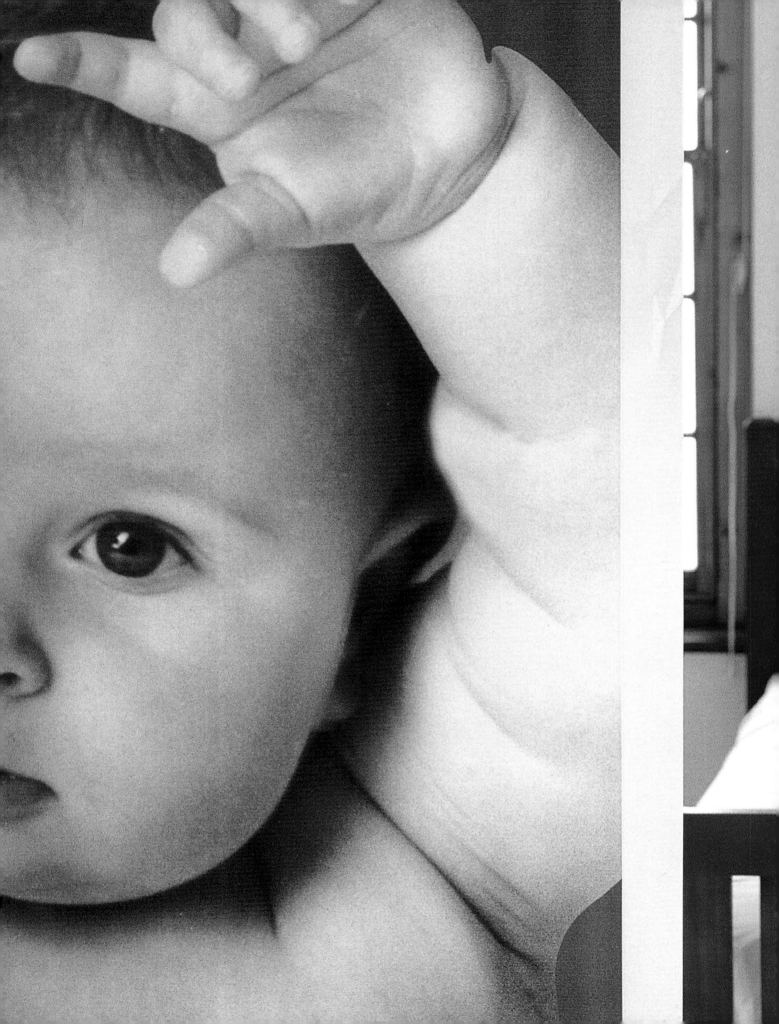

BLOW UP YOUR FAVOURITE BABY

PHOTOGRAPH AND TURN IT INTO

A ROOM DIVIDER. COPY THE SAME

IMAGE ONTO BED LINEN –

ANDY WARHOL STYLE.

SKIN DEEP

SPECIAL PHOTOGRAPHS SHOULD GET THE BIG TREATMENT –

HAVE THEM PRINTED ONTO CANVAS AND BE SURE TO SEAL THE

IMAGE IF YOU INTEND TO USE IT IN THE BATHROOM.

CONCERTINA COLLAGE

THIS COLLAGE OF FAMILY PHOTOGRAPHS AND MEMORIES

MAKES AN INTERESTING ALTERNATIVE TO A CLUSTER OF

BITTY FRAMES.

MIRROR, MIRROR ...

TAKE THE EDGE OFF AN IMPOSING MIRROR BY LAYERING IT

WITH HOLIDAY SNAPS. SUCTION HOOKS AND CABLE

SYSTEMS ALLOW YOU TO USE YOUR MIRROR AS A PINBOARD.

ABOVE: WE ALL GATHER IMAGES AND PHOTOGRAPHS THAT

WE LOVE. CAPTURE YOURS BY PRINTING THEM ONTO PLACE

MATS. DO IT ON A3 BROWN PAPER AND DISCARD AFTER THE

MEAL OR LAMINATE IT FOR POSTERITY.

PICTURE THIS

LEFT: USE SIMPLE GRAPHIC IMAGES FOR A POWERFUL EFFECT.

SNOW GLOBES ARE FUN AND CLEVER CONVERSATION OPENERS. THEY LOOK

JUST AS GOOD ON THE MANTELPIECE AS THEY DO NEXT TO THE IMAC. USE

THEM AT A DINNER PARTY TO INDICATE PLACE SETTINGS WITH PHOTO

IMAGES INSTEAD OF NAMES. SNOW GLOBES ARE DESIGNED IN SUCH A

WAY THAT PHOTOGRAPHS OR MESSSAGES CAN BE SLIPPED INTO THE

GLOBE FROM THE BASE BY TURNING THE GLOBE UPSIDE DOWN AND

REMOUNTING THE DISC. INSERT PHOTOGRAPHS OR MESSAGES ON BOTH

SIDES OF THE DISC AND REPLACE.

SIX

TEA LIGHTS

light *n.* anything that illuminates,
such as a lamp or candle

light up *vb.* (*adv.*) to make or
become cheerful or animated

ABOVE: TURN ANY GLASS JARS INTO LANTERNS AND CLUSTER TOGETHER FOR IMPACT.

RIGHT: SPRINKLE GLITTER ON A SHEET OF PAPER, PAINT THE TEA LIGHT'S METAL CASING WITH A COAT OF PVA CRAFT GLUE AND ROLL IN GLITTER.

LINE UP TEA LIGHTS IN DISPOSABLE COLOURED

GLASSES. CHOOSE A COLOUR TO SUIT YOUR

MOOD AND CHANGE THE COLOUR AS YOU

CHANGE YOUR MOOD.

FIRE LIGHT, FIRE BRIGHT

TEA LIGHTS ARE INEXPENSIVE, INDEPENDENT AND INDISPENSABLE IN TODAY'S HOME. THESE LITTLE CANDLES CAN STAND ON THEIR OWN OR GIVE THEIR MAGIC GLOW TO ANY HOLDER WHEN POPPED INSIDE ONE. REMEMBER, IT'S STILL A CANDLE WITH A FLAME, SO IT'S BEST NOT LEFT ALONE AND SHOULD ONLY BURN IN COMPANY.

FILL HOT DOG BAGS WITH WHITE RIVER SAND TO ANCHOR THEM, THEN PLACE THE TEA LIGHT IN THE CENTRE TO AVOID THE BAGS CATCHING FIRE.

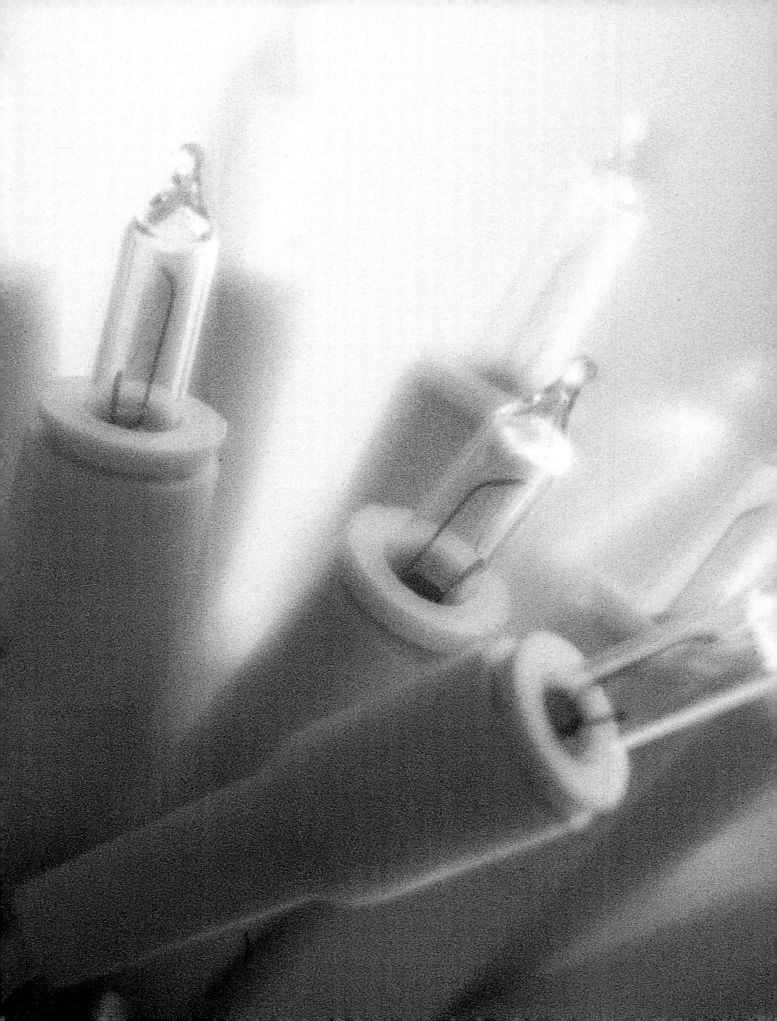

SEVEN

FAIRY LIGHTS

fairy lights *pl. n.* small coloured electric bulbs strung together and used for decoration, esp. on a Christmas tree

fairyland *n.* a fantasy world, esp. one resulting from a person's wild imaginings

TO MAKE A CANISTER LIGHT, SIMPLY

PUNCH A HOLE INTO THE LID OF AN

EMPTY FILM CONTAINER AND PUSH THE

FAIRY GLOBE THROUGH. YOU NEED ONE

CANISTER PER GLOBE, SO START SAVING

NOW OR COLLECT THE REST FROM YOUR

NEAREST FILM-PROCESSING LAB.

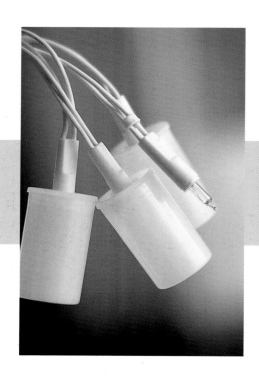

CONTAINED

MAGIC

THIS PAGE: FILL ANY DISCARDED *OBJET* WITH FAIRY

LIGHTS AND IT BECOMES A DESIRED *OBJET*.

RIGHT: A HONEYCOMB LIGHT WORKS WELL AS

A ROOM DIVIDER.

PAPER LANTERNS

USE A STANLEY KNIFE TO CUT A CROSS INTO THE BASES

OF TINY COOKIE CUPS. PUSH THROUGH THE BULB OF A

FAIRY LIGHT TO MAKE A PAPER LANTERN, THEN DRAPE IT

AROUND A MIRROR OR ABOVE THE BED.

MAGIC IN FAIRYLAND

CREATE YOUR OWN MAGICAL ARTWORK: SIMPLY PUNCH HOLES IN

A CLEAN CANVAS AND PUSH FAIRY LIGHT BULBS THROUGH. IT'S A

GOOD IDEA TO LEAVE THE LIGHTS ON WHEN PUSHING THEM

THROUGH TO ENSURE THAT THE CONNECTIONS ARE INTACT. FAIRY

LIGHTS HAVE A LOW VOLTAGE AND ARE HARMLESS.

LIGHT LINE

NEON-LIKE ROPE LIGHTS ARE SOLD PER METRE AND CAN BE INSTALLED ANYWHERE WITH SILICONE GLUE. UNLIKE NEON LIGHTS THE ROPE LIGHT IS FLEXIBLE: YOU CAN BEND IT, CUT IT, CONNECT SEVERAL LENGTHS TOGETHER AND MOULD IT INTO ANY SHAPE YOU LIKE. THEY'RE GREAT FOR STAIRCASES AND DARK PASSAGES AND YOU CAN EVEN TAKE THEM RIGHT AROUND THE ROOM ON SKIRTING BOARDS FOR A COSY GLOW. ALTERNATIVELY YOU CAN SPIRAL A BLUE ROPE LIGHT ABOVE YOUR BED TO MATCH YOUR MOOD. THE POSSIBILITIES ARE ENDLESS!

D A T A B A S E

This book is not meant to motivate you to spend money or send you on a shopping spree. It was written to inspire you and to make you look at everyday objects with different eyes.

Most of the items used to illustrate the ideas were designed as packaging, which was collected or rescued from garbage cans. We've often stumbled across items in hardware and speciality stores that inspired us to come up with new ideas, but these items are basic and available countrywide.

Here are the addresses of manufacturers and suppliers for the impatient decorators who cannot wait until they've collected their own resources. Please keep in mind that some of these companies do not supply directly to the public, or require minimum orders, but they will direct you to a stockist in your area. Alternatively, you can ask to purchase reject material. The product may have been rejected for the purpose it was designed for because of a slight imperfection, but for décor purposes it is perfect.

UNITED KINGDOM

Accessories/Miscellaneous

Designers Guild
267–277 Kings Road
London
SW3 5EN
Telephone: 0207 351 5775
Telephone: 0845 602 1189 (mail order)
Website: www.designersguild.com

For fabric and wallpaper, bedroom, bathroom and kitchen accessories

Farlows
5 Pall Mall
London
SW1Y 5NP
Telephone: 020 7839 2423
Fax: 020 7839 8959
Website: www.farlows.co.uk

For fishing accessories

The General Trading Company
2 Symons Street
Sloane Square
London
SW3 2TJ
Telephone: 020 7730 0411
Fax: 020 7823 5426
Website: www.general-trading.co.uk

For bedroom, bathroom and kitchen accessories

The London Metal Centre
175 Honor Oak Road
London
SE23 3RN
Telephone: 020 8291 7298
Fax: 020 8291 4282
Call or fax the above numbers to place an order, or for details of their Beckenham based factory outlet.

For metal sheeting and cable supplies

Muji
Telephone: 020 7323 2208
Call the above number to find your nearest store.

For Japanese goods – from furniture to household items, clothes, accessories and storage boxes

Neal's Yard Remedies
15 Neal's Yard
Covent Garden
London
WC2 9DP
Telephone: 020 7379 7222
Telephone: 0161 831 7875 (mail order)
Website: www.nealsyardremedies.com

For scented oils

Next Home (mail order)
Telephone: 0845 600 7000
Website: www.next.co.uk
Call the above number for mail order.

Ocean
2 Trevelyan Road
London
SW17 9LR
Telephone: 0870 242 6283 (mail order)
Website: www.oceancatalogue.com

For bedroom, bathroom and kitchen accessories

The Pier
Telephone: 020 7814 5020
Telephone: 020 7814 5004 (mail order)
Call the above numbers to find your nearest
store or for mail order.

Candles/Candle accessories

Candle Makers Supplies
28 Blythe Road
London
W14 0HA
Telephone: 0207 602 4031

The Candle Shop
30 The Market
Covent Garden
London
WC2E 8RE
Telephone: 020 7379 4220
Website: www.candlesontheweb.co.uk

The Candle Shop
50 New Kings Road
Fulham
London
SW6 4LS
Telephone: 020 7836 9815

The Pier
See contact details above.

Wax Lyrical
Telephone: 020 8561 0235 (Head Office)
Website: www.waxlyrical.co.uk
Call the above number to find your nearest store.

Contemporary furniture

Aero
96 Westbourne Grove
London
W2 5AT
Telephone: 020 7221 1950
Fax: 020 7221 2555
Website: www.aero-furniture.com

Aero
347–349 King's Road
Chelsea
London
SW3 5ES
Telephone: 020 7351 0511
Fax: 020 7351 0522

The Conran Shop
Michelin House
81 Fulham Road
London
SW3 6RD
Telephone: 020 7589 7401
Fax: 020 7823 7015
Website: www.conran.co.uk

The Conran Shop
55 Marylebone High Street
London
W1M 3AE
Telephone: 020 7723 2223
Fax: 020 7535 3205

The Conran Collection
12 Conduit Street
London
W1R 9TG
Telephone: 020 7399 0710
Fax: 020 7399 0711

Designers Guild
See contact details on page 117.

Habitat International
The Heal's Building
196 Tottenham Court Road
London
W1P 9LD
Telephone: 020 7255 2545
Fax: 020 7255 6004
Website: www.habitat.co.uk
Call or fax the above numbers to find your
local store.

Heal's
196 Tottenham Court Road
London
W1P 9LD
Telephone: 020 7636 1666
Website: www.heals.co.uk

Heal's
243 King's Road
Chelsea
London
SW3 5UA
Telephone: 020 7349 8411

Heal's
Tunsgate
Guildford
Surrey
GU1 3QU
Telephone: 01483 576715

Heal's
49–51 Eden Street
Kingston Upon Thames
Surrey
KT1 1BW
Telephone: 020 8614 5900

Ikea
Telephone: 020 8208 5607
Website: www.ikea.co.uk
Call the above number for store information
and to order.

Ikea Birmingham
Park Lane
Wednesbury
West Midlands
WS10 9SF
Telephone: 0121 526 5232

Ikea Brent Park
2 Drury Way
North Circular Road
London
NW10 0TH
Telephone: 020 8208 5600

Ikea Bristol
Eastgate Shopping Centre
Eastville
Bristol
BS5 6NW
Telephone: 0117 927 6001

Ikea Croydon
(The Old Power Station)
Valley Park
Purley Way
Croydon
CR0 4UZ
Telephone: 020 8208 5601

Ikea Edinburgh
Straiton Road
Loanhead
Midlothian
EH20 9PW
Telephone: 0131 448 0500

Ikea Gateshead
Metro Park West
Gateshead
Tyne and Wear
NE11 9XS
Telephone: 0191 461 0202

Ikea Leeds
Holden Ing Way
Birstall
Batley
WF17 9AE
Telephone: 01924 423296

Ikea Nottingham
Ikea Way
Goltbrook
Nottingham
NG16 2RP
Telephone: 0115 938 6888

Ikea Thurrock
(Lakeside Retail Park)
Heron Way
West Thurrock
Essex
RM20 3WJ

Ikea Warrington
Gemini Retail Park
910 Europa Boulevard
Warrington
WA5 5TY
Telephone: 01925 655889

Muji
See contact details on page 117.

Next Home (mail order)
See contact details on page 117.

The Pier
See contact details on page 118.

Purves & Purves – Furniture and Accessories
220–224 Tottenham Court Road
London
W1T 7QE
Telephone: 0207 580 8223
Fax: 0207 580 8244
Website: www.purves.co.uk

Fabrics/Soft furnishings

Designers Guild
See contact details on page 117.

John Lewis plc
Oxford Street
London
W1A 1EX
Telephone: 020 7629 7711
Website: www.johnlewis.com
Call the above number to find your nearest store.

Liberty plc
210–220 Regent Street
London
W1R 6AH
Telephone: 020 7734 1234
Fax: 020 7573 9876
Website: www.liberty.co.uk

Marks & Spencer
173 Oxford Street
London
W1R 1TA
Telephone: 020 7437 7722
Website: www.marksandspencer.com
For details of local stores, call head office on
020 7268 1234.

Next Home (mail order)
See contact details on page 117.

Selfridges
400 Oxford Street
London
W1A 1AB
Telephone: 020 7629 1234
Website: www.selfridges.com

General hardware

B & Q
Telephone: 0845 309 3099
Website: www.diy.co.uk
Call the above number to find your nearest store.

Focus Do It All
Telephone: 0800 436436
Website: www.focusdoitall.co.uk
Call the above number to find your nearest store.

Great Mills
Telephone: 0800 052 4404
Website: www.greatmills.co.uk
Call the above number to find your nearest store.

Homebase
Telephone: 020 8784 6555
Website: www.homebase.co.uk
Call the above number to find your nearest store.

Glassware

Cargo Home Shop
Telephone: 08705 134950
Telephone: 01844 261800 (head office)
Website: www.cargo.co.uk
Call the above numbers to find your nearest store.

Designers Guild
See contact details on page 117.

The Pier
200 Tottenham Court Road
London
W1P 7PL
Telephone: 020 7637 7001 or 020 7814 5020
Website: www.pier.co.uk
Call the above number for details of other branches or for mail order.

Kitchenware

Divertimenti
45–47 Wigmore Street
London
W1U 1PS
Telephone: 020 7935 0689
Website: www.divertimenti.co.uk

Divertimenti
139–141 Fulham Road
London
SW3 6SD
Telephone: 020 7581 8065

Ikea
See contact details on pages 119–120.

John Lewis plc
See contact details on page 121.

Muji
See contact details on page 117.

Selfridges
See contact details on page 121.

Lighting

Aero
See contact details on page 118.

Christopher Wray Lighting
591–593 Kings Road
London
SW6 2YW
Telephone: 020 7751 8701
Fax: 020 7751 8732
Website: www.christopherwray.co.uk
Call the above number for details of other branches.

The Conran Shop
See contact details on pages 118–119.

Habitat International
See contact details on page 119.

Heal's
See contact details on page 119.

Ikea
See contact details on pages 119–120.

Purves & Purves – Furniture and Accessories
See contact details on page 121.

Paint supplies

Crown Paint
Akzo Nobel Decorative Coatings Ltd
Crown House
Hollins Road
Darwin
Lancashire
BB3 0BG
Telephone: 01254 704951
Website: www.crownpaint.co.uk
Call the above number to find your local stockist.

Dulux Paint
Telephone: 01753 550555
Website: www.dulux.co.uk
Call the above number to find your local stockist.

Fired Earth
Telephone: 01295 814315 (Head Office Sales)
Website: www.firedearth.co.uk
Call the above number to find your local stockist.

Leyland Paint
Huddersfield Road
Birstall
Batley
West Yorkshire
WF17 9XA
Telephone: 01924 354000
Website: www.sigmakalon.com

Photocopy shops

Kall Kwik
(Photocopy shops nationwide aimed at both the business and individual client)
Telephone: 01895 872000
Website: www.kallkwik.co.uk
Call the above number to find your nearest store, or visit the website.

Stationery suppliers

Muji
See contact details on page 117.

Office World
Telephone: 0800 500024
Call the above number to find your nearest store.

Paperchase
213 Tottenham Court Road
London
W1P 9AF
Telephone: 020 7467 6200 (head office)
Telephone: 0161 839 1500 (mail order)
Website: www.paperchase.co.uk
Call the above numbers to find your nearest store or for mail order.

Ryman the Stationer
Telephone: 020 8569 3000 (head office)
Website: www.ryman.co.uk
Call the above number to find your nearest store.

NEW ZEALAND

Furniture

Backhouse Interiors
1 Kenwyn Street
Parnell
Auckland
Telephone: 0-9-377 4708

Country Road Homewares
Telephone: 0800 105 655 for stores

Matisse International Furniture
99 The Strand
Parnell
Auckland
Telephone: 0-9-302 2284

23 Allen Street
Wellington
Telephone: 0-4-801 2121

Limited Editions
258–262 Thorndon Quay
Wellington
Telephone: 0-4-473 4220
Fax: 0-4-471 2892
E-mail: design@limitededitions.co.nz

Cavit and Company
547a Parnell Road
Parnell
Auckland
Telephone: 0-9-358 3771
Website: www.cavitco.co.nz

Freedom Furniture
Branches nationwide
Freephone: 0800 373 336

Paints

Resene Paints Limited
Telephone: 0-4-577 0500
Fax: 0-4-577 0664
Technical Advice: 0800-RESENE (800-737-363)
Website: www.resene.co.nz

Décor and accessories

Askew Design Store
195 Parnell Road
Parnell
Auckland
Telephone: 0-9-358 1825

Flooring

Jacobsen Creative Surfaces
Freephone: 0800 800 460

Branches:
228 Orakei Rd
Remuera
Auckland
Telephone: 0-9-524 1460

96 Hutt St
Kaiwharawhara
Wellington
Telephone: 0-4-472 8528

314 Manchester St
Christchurch
Telephone: 0-3-366 4153

Firth Industries
Branches nationwide
Freephone: 0800 800 576

Placemakers
Branches nationwide
Freephone: 0800 425 2269

Lighting

Light Ideas Ltd

Branches:
Auckland: 0-9-444 4220
Christchurch: 0-3-365 5370
Dunedin: 0-3-477 7549
Hamilton: 0-7-834 0320
Invercargill: 0-3-214 0481
Napier: 0-6-834 0184
Nelson: 0-3-548 9384
New Plymouth: 0-6-758 8170
Palmerston North: 0-6-358 8300
Tauranga: 0-7-578 7177
Wellington: 0-4-473 0200
Whangarei: 0-9-438 4122

ECC Lighting & ECC Living
39 Nugent Street
Grafton
Auckland
Telephone: 0-9-379 9680

61–63 Thorndon Quay
Wellington
Telephone: 0-4-473 3456

Targetti
Telephone: 0-9-302 0548 for stockists

General

The Warehouse
Branches nationwide
Website: www.thewarehouse.co.nz

ACKNOWLEDGEMENTS

THANK YOU!

To **Ingo Maurer,** whose 'Zettel'z' chandelier was the inspiration for chapter two. Don't you just love his 'Lucellino' with goose feather wings on pages 38 and 39? See also page 75 where we framed one of the notes from the 'Zettel'z' chandelier.

To **Elliott Erwitt,** whose dog postcards appear on pages 82 and 91. His boxed postcard collection is called DogDOGS.

To **Stephen Inggs,** for the use of his artwork on pages 34, 37, 84, 92 and 107. If you love them, you can own them!

To **Dook,** for the use of 'Nikki' on page 89 from his book *Skin and Bone*.

To **Michael Methven,** for the use of his papier-mâché buffalo light fitting on page 71.

To **Lindi Sales,** for the use of her family collage on page 90.

To **Francesco Sardella,** for the use of his photograph of dogs on page 83.

To **Annel Botha,** for the use of baby Elke Hansen's photograph on pages 80, 86 and 87.

To **Sonja Zimberlin,** for the use of her painting on page 52.

To **Russel Jones** from Scan Shop, for scans and prints for chapter five.

To **Rosalind Stone**, public relations officer for Kohler, for introducing us to their wonderful products.

To **Massimo Cecconi,** for the use of his photograph of folded paper on page 43.

First published in 2001 by
New Holland Publishers (UK) Ltd
Garfield House
86–88 Edgware Road
London W2 2EA
United Kingdom
www.newhollandpublishers.com

1 2 3 4 5 6 7 8 9 10

Editor: Joy Clack
Copy editor: Kerryn du Preez
Designer: Petal Palmer
Design assistant: Natascha Adendorff
Photographer: Massimo Cecconi
Photographic assistant: Francesco Sardella
Production assistant: Alison Faure

Reproduction by Hirt & Carter Cape (Pty) Ltd
Printed and bound by Sing Cheong Printing Company Limited

ISBN 1 84330 033 8

FAST
DÉCOR